Passport to Paris

Alison Gardner

The author would like to thank Kate Amis for her invaluable help and advice whilst researching this title.

Published 2009 by
A & C Black Publishers Ltd.
36 Soho Square, London, W1D 3QY
www.acblack.com

ISBN HB 978-1-4081-1210-6
    PB 978-1-4081-1295-3

Series consultant: Gill Matthews

This book is produced using paper that is made from wood grown in managed, sustainable forests. It is natural, renewable and recyclable. The logging and manufacturing processes conform to the environmental regulations of the country of origin.

Produced for A & C Black by Calcium.
Printed and bound in China by C&C Offset Printing Co.

All the internet addresses given in this book were correct at the time of going to press. The author and publishers regret any inconvenience caused if addresses have changed or sites have ceased to exist, but can accept no responsibility for any such changes.

Acknowledgements
The publishers would like to thank the following for their kind permission to reproduce their photographs:
Cover: Shutterstock. **Pages:** Corbis: Christian Liewig/Tempsport 18c; Istockphoto: Leon Bonaventura throughout, Ilker Canikligil 10c, Michael DeLeon 8t, Yury Khupchenko 6, Michel Mory 7t; Rex Features: Sipa Press 9t; Shutterstock: Peter Blazek 13, Cynoclub 14tr, S Duffett 20t, Keith Levit 11, Thierry Maffeis 17, Michael Mattox 15, Clara Natoli 12b, Marc Pagani Photography 19t, Pandapaw 5t, Andrey Shadrin throughout, Ljupco Smokovski 21, Thomas Sztanek 16b. **Map:** Geoff Ward 4b.

Contents

Welcome To Paris

Paris is the capital city of France. This means that the **government** is based here. The people who live in Paris are called Parisians. Paris is an **historic** city with many grand buildings that were built in the 17th century – more than 300 years ago!

My name is Jean-Paul and I am going to show you around my city. I have lived here all my life. I love living in Paris because there is so much to see and do!

• Paris

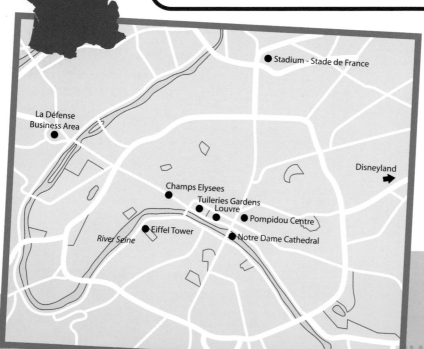

• Stadium - Stade de France

La Défense Business Area •

Disneyland ➡

Champs Elysees •

Tuileries Gardens
• Louvre
• Pompidou Centre
• Eiffel Tower
River Seine
• Notre Dame Cathedral

This map of Paris shows all the main sites of interest.

Green spaces

Despite being a built-up city, Paris has many fine parks and gardens. These range from the formal *Tuileries* to the wilder *Bois de Boulogne* where Parisians and visitors can walk, cycle, ride horses, canoe, and fish. *Parc de la Villette* is Paris's largest green, where you can find concert halls, cinemas, and theatres. It is multicultural and always **festive**.

The *Tuileries* gardens were built as royal pleasure gardens, filled with fruit and flowers.

City beach

For one month in the summer, sand is deposited along a 3-km (2-mile) stretch of the River Seine. Known as the *Paris Plage*, it is very popular. Beach chairs and sun-loungers, shady palm trees, and temporary swimming pools make it a cool haven in a hot, dusty city.

Did you know?
On average, 25 million **tourists** visit Paris every year.

Living In The City

Lots of people live in the centre of Paris so it's quite crowded. We have a large number of students and many foreign residents. Some people come to Paris to study and then decide to work here, because they like the Parisian life so much.

Places to live

Everyone needs a place to live and in Paris there are lots of different types of homes. In the centre of Paris there is not enough space for everyone to have a big house, so most people have **apartments**.

City views

Most of the apartments in the centre of Paris are over 200 years old. My grandparents live in an old apartment. They have a balcony with lots of plants and really good views of the River Seine!

Living in a city apartment means you are close to all the shops and cafés.

Suburban living

In the **suburbs** of Paris, people live in houses. I live with my parents in a house in the suburbs. Out here, there are many gardens. In the centre of Paris, houses with gardens are expensive. On the outskirts of Paris, tall buildings provide plenty of homes for the growing population.

Did you know?
Many people who live and work in Paris come from other countries, for example Algeria and Senegal.

Welcome to my home! I live in a house like the one above.

Going To a City School

I go to a primary school in Paris. The French word for school is *école*. Our lessons are a lot like yours but we also take lessons in English and Spanish from the age of five. This means that by the time we leave our *école* we are very good at languages!

We also take lessons in **civic education**, which teaches us how to be good **citizens**.

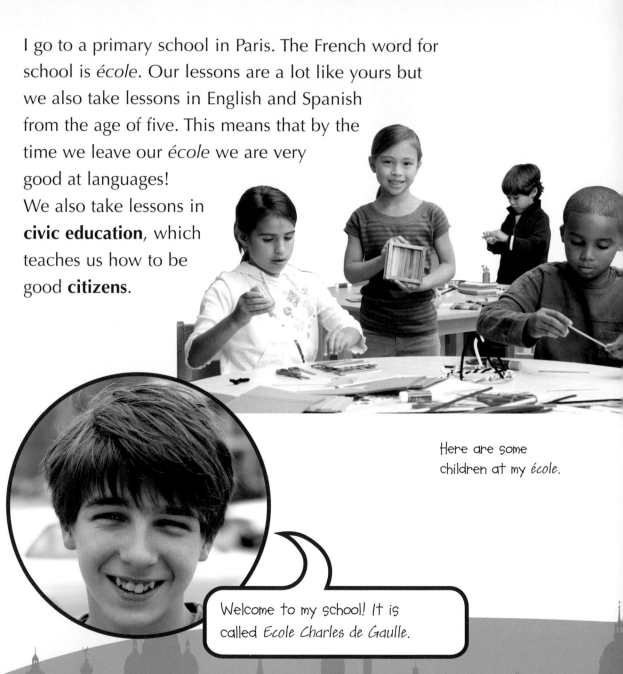

Here are some children at my *école*.

Welcome to my school! It is called *Ecole Charles de Gaulle*.

Secondary school

My sister Marie is older than me. She goes to a secondary school here in Paris. The French word for secondary school is *lycée*. Marie goes to a large *lycée* with more than 2,000 students! You can see her timetable below. On Wednesdays there are no lessons, but the school is open for sports practice.

Students at the *lycée* do not wear a school uniform.

Monday	Tuesday	Wednesday
8a.m. – 2p.m.	8a.m. – 2p.m.	school closed
Thursday	Friday	Saturday
8a.m. – 2p.m.	8a.m. – 2p.m.	8a.m. – 12 midday

Marie really enjoys going to the *lycée*, but they have a lot of homework to do. If she doesn't pass her exams in the summer she is not allowed to move up a class the following year. When she gets older, she is hoping to study history of art at the famous Sorbonne University.

Did you know?
University education is free in France, but you must pass a very hard exam called the *Baccalauréat* to be given a place.

Working in the City

Nearly everyone living in the city goes to work — let me tell you about where my parents work.

There are 2.5 million people living and working in the city of Paris. Paris is an important world centre for banks and other big businesses. *La Défense* is the business area of Paris. Many tourists go to see the 100-m (330-ft) high *Grande Arche* (an office building completed in 1989).

The *Grande Arche* is a huge squared arch that could cover *Notre Dame* **Cathedral**.

Did you know?
La Défense has 150,000 daily workers and is Europe's largest business district.

My mum works in one of these office blocks. She is a translator for an international company. This means she reads documents in French and then writes them out in English so that people from other countries can understand them.

The schools and hospitals in Paris need **skilled** people to work there. My dad works in a large hospital in Paris. He is a nurse and looks after patients in the Accident and Emergency department.

In the centre of Paris many people have jobs in the **tourist industry**. This means that they help people visiting Paris from other countries.

A waiter in a Parisian restaurant serves tourists.

Getting Around the City

Paris is quite a small city, so it doesn't take long to get from one place to another.

The *Métro*

The ***Métro*** train in Paris is quick and cheap and reaches most areas of Paris and the suburbs. The time of day when everyone is going to work is called the rush hour. The *Métro* gets very crowded during rush hour. The best way to travel on the *Métro* is with a *carnet*. This is a book of 10 tickets that costs 11 Euros. It is cheaper than buying separate tickets.

There are lots of different ways to travel around Paris.

The Paris *Métro* has 368 stations.

River bus

The River Seine flows through Paris. The *bâteau* bus travels up and down the river. It is slow and costs more than most other forms of transport in Paris, so it is mainly tourists who use it.

A great way to explore Paris is on foot.

Cycling

Some people like to cycle. Paris has a bicycle sharing system called *Vélib*. People can rent a bicycle, which they pick up and drop off at one of the 750 **locations** in the city.

Walking

Paris has wide pavements and some roads that are closed to cars for most of the day. This makes Paris a pleasant place to walk around.

Did you know?
It only takes about two hours to walk across Paris.

Sightseeing in the City

The most well-known tourist attraction in Paris is the Eiffel Tower. It was finished in 1889 and was built to celebrate the anniversary of the **French Revolution**. From the top of the Eiffel Tower you can see that the city is very big and has been carefully planned. Wide, straight roads link many grand squares together.

There are lots of interesting sights in Paris. Let me show you around!

The Eiffel Tower was only meant to stay for one year, but it is so popular that it is still there 100 years later!

Did you know?
The Eiffel Tower has 1,665 steps and 20,000 light bulbs!

Victor Hugo saves *Notre Dame*!

The most famous cathedral in Paris is called *Notre Dame*. The cathedral is on an island in the middle of the River Seine. About 200 years ago the cathedral was falling down so the city planners decided to destroy it. The French writer Victor Hugo really liked the cathedral. He wrote his book *The Hunchback of Notre Dame* to remind people that the cathedral was worth saving. His plan worked and the cathedral was repaired.

Building work on *Notre Dame* Cathedral began in 1163. That's over 800 years ago!

Disneyland

One of the most popular places to go here is Disneyland Paris, on the outskirts of the city. It is visited by people from all over Europe and the rest of the world.

Shopping in the City

Whatever you want to buy, you can find it in Paris! There are lots of shops that all sell different **products**.

What's in store

The main shopping street in Paris is called the *Champs Elysées*. Here the shops sell expensive items, such as jewellery and fashionable clothes. Lots of companies have their biggest shops on the *Champs Elysées*.

In the centre of Paris you will also find large **department stores** that sell a mixture of items such as food, clothes, toys, and shoes. The most famous department store in Paris is *Galeries Lafayettes*.

Galeries Lafayettes has 96 departments, each selling different products.

Shopping in Paris is great! There are hundreds of different shops from small street markets to huge department stores.

Books

If you enjoy books and magazines, bargains can be found on the second-hand book stalls that line the Left Bank of the River Seine.

Marvellous markets

Parisians enjoy visiting markets to buy their food and clothes. The markets are often in the suburbs of the city. At the food market all the food is fresh and comes from the French countryside. There you can buy seasonal fruit and vegetables, bread and cakes, cheeses, olives, garlic, and much more. At the **antique** markets you can buy beautiful old furniture, ornaments, and jewellery.

Parisians buy more food from markets than supermarkets.

Being Active in the City

Parisians are passionate about football! Paris held and won the World Cup final in 1998. A new **stadium** was built for the competition in the suburbs of the city. It is now used for cup final matches and international matches.

International ball games

Rugby is also a popular sport in Paris. The most successful Parisian team is called *Stade Français*. The French national team is very successful too.

France winning the football World Cup in 1998.

I am a fan of *Paris Saint-Germain*, a football team in Paris.

Cycling and skating

French people also really enjoy cycling. Every year thousands of people line the streets of Paris to watch the *Tour de France*. This is a long cycle race around the country that begins and ends in Paris.

Parisians are also crazy about roller skating! Every Friday night 15,000 roller skaters skate round the centre of Paris. Roads are closed so they can enjoy the wide, empty streets.

Did you know?
Many of the footballers who play for *Paris Saint-Germain* are from other countries including Brazil and Portugal.

Arts in the City

Paris has some of the most famous museums and art galleries in the world! Here you can see paintings and sculptures by well-known artists such as Monet and Leonardo da Vinci.

Museums

Most of the museums are in the historic centre of Paris, near the river. This makes it easy for large numbers of people to get here.

The *Louvre* was first opened to the public in 1793.

Today my grandparents are taking me to the biggest museum in France – the *Louvre*.

The *Louvre*

The *Louvre* is in a beautiful building. It used to be a royal palace. In 1988 a new entrance to the museum was built. It is a giant pyramid made of glass. It looks very different from the old building and some people were against it being built. I think it looks great! Inside, there are over 35,000 **exhibits** from all over the world.

The amazing new entrance to the *Louvre*.

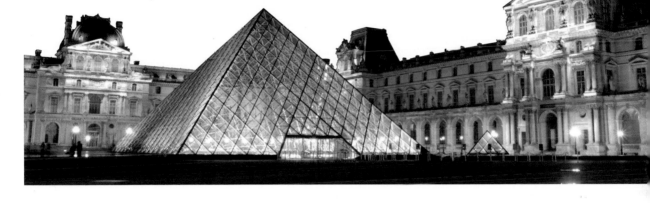

Pompidou Centre

This cultural centre is "inside out" – all its heating pipes, air ducts, and escalators are on the outside of the building! Inside are theatres, galleries, and a cinema. The large square in front is like a stage for street performers who attract huge crowds on a fine day.

Glossary

antique something that was made a long time ago

apartments flats

cathedral a large church

citizens people who live in a particular place

civic education where you learn about your country and how it is run

department stores large shops that sell a wide range of items

exhibits paintings, sculptures, or objects in museums and art galleries

festive fun event that takes place at certain times of the year

French Revolution the revolution in France against the royal family

government a group of people who are in charge of how a country is run

historic something important from the past

locations particular places

Métro underground railway

products items you can buy

skilled experienced, trained well

stadium a large building that holds many people. Usually for football or other sports

suburbs the area of housing that surrounds a city

tourists visitors to a city or place – often from other countries

tourist industry the businesses that help people to visit a city or place

Further Information

Websites

The official website of the Paris Tourist Board can be found at:
www.parisinfo.com

Visit the Eiffel Tower website at:
www.tour-eiffel.fr

Take a look at Disneyland Paris at:
www.disneylandparis.com

Books

The Hunchback of Notre Dame by Victor Hugo, edited by Jan Needle. Walker Books (2006).

City Walks with Kids by Natasha Edwards and Roman Klonek. Universal Books (2008).

The Eiffel Tower by Meg Greene. Blackbirch Press (2003).

This is Paris by Miroslav Sasek. Universe Publishing (2004).

Index